Holiday Hug'ems™

General Information

Many of the products used in this pattern book can be purchased from local craft, fabric and variety stores, or from the Annie's Attic Needlecraft Catalog (see Customer Service information on page 40).

Contents

Scarecrow

SKILL LEVEL

INTERMEDIATE

FINISHED SIZE
16 inches tall sitting

MATERIALS
- Red Heart Super Saver medium (worsted) weight yarn (solids: 7 oz/364 yds/198g; multis: 5 oz/ 244 yds/141g per skein):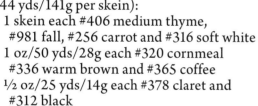
  - 1 skein each #406 medium thyme, #981 fall, #256 carrot and #316 soft white
  - 1 oz/50 yds/28g each #320 cornmeal #336 warm brown and #365 coffee
  - ½ oz/25 yds/14g each #378 claret and #312 black
- Aunt Lydia's Classic size 10 crochet cotton (350 yds per ball):
  - 1 ball #323 melon
- Size 7/1.65mm steel crochet hook
- Size H/8/5mm crochet hook or size needed to obtain gauge
- Tapestry needle
- Sewing needle
- Sewing thread
- 30 x 40-inch piece of light orange flannel or blanket fabric
- Fiberfill
- 7-inch piece of hook-and-loop fastener
- Pompom maker
- Stitch marker

GAUGE
Size H hook and yarn: 4 sc = 1 inch

PATTERN NOTES
Use size H hook with yarn and size 7 hook with crochet cotton.

Join with slip stitch as indicated unless otherwise stated.

Chain-3 at beginning of row or round counts as first double crochet unless otherwise stated.

Work in continuous rounds, do not turn or join unless otherwise stated.

Mark first stitch of each round.

Chain-2 at beginning of row or round counts as first half double crochet unless otherwise stated.

INSTRUCTIONS
BLANKET
Rnd 1: Working around outer edge of fabric, using **size 7 hook** *(see Pattern Notes)*, pushing hook through fabric ¼ inch from edge of fabric and with sts ¼ inch apart, join crochet cotton with sc near 1 corner, *evenly sp (ch 2, sc) across until you have an even number of ch sps along side to next corner, ch 4 for corner, rep from * around, **join** *(see Pattern Notes)* in beg sc. Fasten off.

Rnd 2: With size H hook, join fall with sc in last corner ch sp, 2 sc in same corner ch sp, *sc in each ch sp around with 5 sc in each corner ch sp, 2 sc in same corner ch sp as beg sc, join in beg sc.

Rnd 3: Ch 3 *(see Pattern Notes)*, dc in same st, ch 3, from back of work, sl st in top of last dc worked, dc in same st, sk next st, sl st in next st, sk next st, [(2 dc, ch 3, from back of work, sl st in top of last dc worked, dc in same st) in next st, sk next st, sl st in next st, sk next st] around, skipping extra st or do not sk a st at all so you are working in center corner st, join in 3rd ch of beg ch-3. Fasten off.

SCARECROW
HEAD
Rnd 1: Beg at top, with soft white, ch 2, 6 sc in 2nd ch from hook, **do not join** (see Pattern Notes). (6 sc)

Rnd 2: 2 sc in each st around. (12 sc)

Rnd 3: [Sc in next st, 2 sc in next st] around. (18 sc)

Rnd 4: [Sc in each of next 2 sts, 2 sc in next st] around. (24 sc)

Rnd 5: [2 sc in next st, sc in each of next 3 sts] around. (30 sc)

Rnd 6: [Sc in each of next 4 sts, 2 sc in next st] around. (36 sc)

Rnd 7: [Sc in each of next 5 sts, 2 sc in next st] around. (42 sc)

Rnd 8: Sc in each st around.

Rnd 9: [Sc in each of next 6 sts, 2 sc in next st] around. (48 sc)

Rnd 10: Sc in each st around.

Rnd 11: [Sc in each of next 11 sts, 2 sc in next st] around. (52 sc)

Rnds 12–23: Sc in each st around.

Rnd 24: [Sc in each of next 11 sts, **sc dec** (see Stitch Guide) in next 2 sts] around. Stuff Head. (48 sc)

Rnd 25: [Sc in each of next 4 sts, sc dec in next 2 sts] around. (40 sc)

Rnd 26: [Sc in each of next 3 sts, sc dec in next 2 sts] around. Finish stuffing Head. (32 sc)

Rnd 27: [Sc in each of next 2 sts, sc dec in next 2 sts] around, join in beg sc. Leaving long end, fasten off. (24 sc)

BODY
Rnd 1: Beg at neck of shirt, with carrot, ch 24, sc in first ch to form ring, sc in each ch around, do not join. (24 sc)

Rnd 2: [Sc in next st, 2 sc in next st] around. (36 sc)

Rnd 3: [Sc in each of next 3 sts, 2 sc in next st] around. (45 sc)

Rnd 4: Sc in each st around.

Rnd 5: [Sc in each of next 4 sts, 2 sc in next st] around. (54 sc)

Rnd 6: Sc in each st around.

Rnd 7: [Sc in each of next 8 sts, 2 sc in next st] around. (60 sc)

Rnds 8–16: Sc in each st around. At end of last rnd, fasten off.

PANTS
Rnd 17: Join medium thyme with sc in first st, sc in each st around, join in beg sc.

Rnd 18: Working in **back lps** (see Stitch Guide), ch 1, sc in each st around, do not join.

Rnds 19–34: Sc in each st around.

Rnd 35: [Sc in each of next 4 sts, sc dec in next 2 sts] around. (50 sc)

Rnd 36: [Sc in each of next 3 sts, sc dec in next 2 sts] around. Stuff Body. (40 sc)

Rnd 37: [Sc in each of next 2 sts, sc dec in next 2 sts] around. (30 sc)

Rnd 38: [Sc in each of next 3 sts, sc dec in next 2 sts] around. (24 sc)

Rnd 39: [Sc in each of next 2 sts, sc dec in next 2 sts] around. (18 sc)

Rnd 40: [Sc in next st, sc dec in next 2 sts] around. Finish stuffing Body. (12 sc)

Rnd 41: [Sc dec in next 2 sts] around, join in beg sc. Leaving long end, fasten off. (6 sc)

Weave long end through top of sts of last rnd, pull to close. Secure end.

Using **straight stitch** (see Fig. 2), embroider mouth in shape of smile. Then make small sts at corners and in center of smile. Make 2 small sts between corner and center st on each side as shown in photo.

Fig. 2
Straight Stitch

Using long end on Head, sew Head to top of Body.

NOSE
Row 1: With claret, ch 4, sl st in 2nd ch from hook, sc in next ch, hdc in last ch, turn. *(3 sts)*

Row 2: Ch 2 *(see Pattern Notes)*, hdc in same st, sc in next sc, (sl st, ch 2, sl st) in last st, working in starting ch of opposite side of row 1, sl st in each of next 2 chs, sc in next ch, (hdc, ch 1, sl st) in last ch, working across bottom edge, sl st in end of next 2 rows, sl st in end of same row *(this is the lower right corner of Nose)*. Fasten off.

Sew Nose to rnds 16–20 on Head.

FINISHING
Using **satin stitch** (see Fig. 1), with black, embroider eyes over rnds 13–17 on Head 1¾ inches apart above Nose as shown in photo.

Fig. 1
Satin Stitch

HAIR
Cut 280 strands cornmeal, each 9 inches in length. Holding 2 strands tog, fold in half, insert hook in st on Head, pull fold through, pull ends through fold. Pull to tighten.

Attach 20 strands across top of Head for bangs, 30 strands down each side of Head to rnd 20 to frame face and 60 strands around back of Head in rnd 20. Trim ends as needed.

ARM
MAKE 2.
Rnd 1: Beg at top, with carrot, ch 20, sc in first ch to form ring, sc in each ch around, **do not join**. *(20 sc)*

Rnds 2–28: Sc in each st around. At end of last rnd, join in beg sc.

CUFF
Rnd 29: Working in **front lps** (see Stitch Guide), ch 1, sc in each of first 3 sts, 2 sc in next st, [sc in each of next 3 sts, 2 sc in next st] around. *(25 sc)*

Rnd 30: Sc in each st around, join in beg sc. Fasten off.

HAND
MAKE 2.
Rnd 1: Working in rem lps of rnd 28, join soft white with sc in first st, sc in each st around, **do not join**. *(20 sc)*

Rnd 2: Working in back lps, sc in each of first 3 sts, [2 sc in next st, sc in next st] 4 times, sc in each of last 9 sts. *(24 sts)*

Rnds 3–7: Sc in each st around.

Rnd 8: [Sc in each of next 2 sts, sc dec in next 2 sts] around. *(18 sc)*

Rnd 9: [Sc in next st, sc dec in next 2 sts] around. *(12 sc)*

Rnd 10: [Sc dec in next 2 sts] around. Leaving long end, fasten off. *(6 sc)*

Weave long end through top of sts on last rnd, pull to close. Secure end.

Stuff Arm lightly, leaving the top 2 inches unstuffed.

Flatten rnd 1 and sew closed.

Sew Arms to sides of Body as shown in photo.

LEG
MAKE 2.
Rnds 1–30: Using medium thyme, rep rnds 1–30 of Arm.

FOOT
MAKE 2.
Rnds 1–10: With coffee, rep rnds 1–10 of Hand.

Weave long end through top of sts on last rnd, pull to close. Secure end.

Stuff Leg lightly, leaving the top 2 inches unstuffed.

Flatten rnd 1 and sew closed.

Sew Legs to sides of Body as shown in photo.

STRAW
Cut 160 strands of cornmeal, each 6 inches in length. Holding 2 strands tog, fold in half, insert hook in st, pull fold through, pull ends through fold. Pull to tighten.

Attach Straw in rem lps of rnd 1 on Hands and Feet. Trim ends.

OVERALL BIB
Row 1: Working in rem lp on rnd 17 at waist with Head facing away, working in center 18 sts across front, join medium thyme with sc in first st, sc in each of next 17 sts, turn. *(18 sc)*

Rows 2–6: Ch 1, sc in each st across, turn.

Rows 7 & 8: Ch 1, sc in first st, sc dec in next 2 sts, sc in each st across to last 3 sts, sc dec in next 2 sts, sc in last st, turn. *(14 sc at end of last row)*

Row 9: Ch 1, sc in first st, sc dec in next 2 sts, sc in each st across to last 3 sts, sc dec in next 2 sts, sc in last st. Fasten off. *(12 sc)*

OVERALL STRAP
MAKE 2.
Row 1: With medium thyme, ch 3, sc in 2nd ch from hook and in last ch, turn. *(2 sc)*

Rows 2–32: Ch 1, sc in each st across, turn.

Row 33: Ch 1, (sc, dc) in first st, (dc, ch 2, sc) in last st. Fasten off.

Sew row 1 of Straps to rnd 18 at center back.

Sew last row of Straps to row 31 in front as shown in photo.

FINISHING
Using **French knots** *(see Fig. 3)*, with warm brown, embroider 1 button on end of each Strap in front.

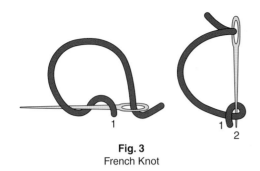

Fig. 3
French Knot

COLLAR
With carrot, ch 33, 3 dc in 4th ch from hook, dc in each of next 28 chs, (3 dc, ch 2, sl st) in last ch. Fasten off.

Place Collar around neck with ends at center front. Sew in place.

BOW TIE
Row 1: With warm brown, ch 5, sc in 2nd ch from hook and in each ch across, turn. *(4 sc)*

Row 2: Ch 1, sc in each st across, turn.

Row 3: Ch 1, sc dec in first 2 sts, sc dec in last 2 sts, turn. *(2 sc)*

Row 4: Ch 1, sc dec in 2 sts, turn. *(1 sc)*

Row 5: Ch 1, 2 sc in st, turn. *(2 sc)*

Row 6: Ch 1, 2 sc in first st, 2 sc in last st, turn. *(4 sc)*

Row 7: Ch 1, sc in each st across, turn.

Row 8: Ch 1, sc in each st across. Fasten off.

Tack center of Bow Tie to center front of Collar.

PATCH
MAKE 2.
Row 1: With warm brown, ch 4, sc in 2nd ch from hook and in each ch across, turn. *(3 sc)*

Row 2: Ch 1, sc in each st across, turn.

Row 3: Ch 1, sc in each st across. Fasten off.

With soft white, sew Patches to knee area on each Leg as shown in photo.

With sewing thread, sew 2-inch piece of hook-and-loop fastener to outer right Hand and right Foot, and to inner left Hand and left Foot.

HAT
Rnd 1: With medium thyme, ch 4, sl st in first ch to form ring, **ch 2** *(see Pattern Notes)*, 11 hdc in ring, join in 2nd ch of beg ch-2. *(12 hdc)*

Rnd 2: Ch 2, hdc in same st, 2 hdc in each st around, join in 2nd ch of beg ch-2. *(24 hdc)*

Rnd 3: Ch 2, 2 hdc in next st, [hdc in next st, 2 hdc in next st] around, join in 2nd ch of beg ch-2. *(36 hdc)*

Rnd 4: Ch 2, hdc in each of next 2 sts, 2 hdc in next st, [hdc in each of next 3 sts, 2 hdc in next st] around, join in 2nd ch of beg ch-2. *(45 hdc)*

Rnd 5: Ch 2, hdc in each of next 3 sts, 2 hdc in next st, [hdc in each of next 4 sts, 2 hdc in next st] around, join in 2nd ch of beg ch-2. *(54 hdc)*

Rnd 6: Ch 2, hdc in each of next 7 sts, 2 hdc in next st, [hdc in each of next 8 sts, 2 hdc in next st] around, join in 2nd ch of beg ch-2. *(60 hdc)*

Rnd 7: Ch 2, hdc in each of next 8 sts, 2 hdc in next st, [hdc in each of next 9 sts, 2 hdc in next st] around, join in 2nd ch of beg ch-2. *(66 hdc)*

Rnds 8–13: Ch 2, hdc in each st around, join in 2nd ch of beg ch-2.

Rnd 14: Ch 2, hdc in each of next 8 sts, **hdc dec** *(see Stitch Guide)* in next 2 sts, [hdc in each of next 9 sts, hdc dec in next 2 sts] around, join in 2nd ch of beg ch-2. *(60 hdc)*

BRIM
Rnd 15: Ch 2, 2 hdc in next st, [hdc in next st, 2 hdc in next st] around, join in 2nd ch of beg ch-2. *(90 hdc)*

Rnd 16: Ch 2, hdc in each st around, join in 2nd ch of beg ch-2. Fasten off.

Sew Hat to top of Head as shown in photo. ■

Uncle Sam Bear

SKILL LEVEL

INTERMEDIATE

FINISHED SIZE
17 inches tall sitting, including Hat

MATERIALS
- Red Heart Super Saver medium (worsted) weight yarn (7 oz/ 364 yds/198g per skein):
  1 skein #385 royal
  3 oz/150yds/85g each #311 white, #319 cherry red and #336 warm brown
  ½ oz/25 yds/14g #312 black
- Aunt Lydia's Classic size 10 crochet cotton (350 yds per ball):
  1 ball #487 dark royal
- Size 7/1.65mm steel crochet hook
- Size H/8/5mm crochet hook or size needed to obtain gauge
- Tapestry needle
- Sewing needle
- Sewing thread
- 30 x 40-inch piece of blue flannel or blanket fabric
- Fiberfill
- 4-inch piece of hook-and-loop fastener
- Stitch marker

GAUGE
Size H hook and yarn: 4 sc = 1 inch

PATTERN NOTES
Use size H hook with yarn and size 7 hook with crochet cotton.

Join with slip stitch as indicated unless otherwise stated.

Work in continuous rounds, do not turn or join unless otherwise stated.

Mark first stitch of each round.

Chain-2 at beginning of row or round counts as first half double crochet unless otherwise stated.

INSTRUCTIONS
BLANKET
Rnd 1: Working around outer edge of fabric, using **size 7 hook** (*see Pattern Notes*), pushing hook through fabric ¼ inch from edge of fabric and with sts ¼ inch apart, join crochet cotton with sc near 1 corner, *evenly sp (ch 2, sc) across until you have an even number of ch sps along side to next corner, ch 4 for corner, rep from * around, **join** (*see Pattern Notes*) in beg sc. Fasten off.

Rnd 2: With **size H hook** (*see Pattern Notes*), join royal with sc in any corner ch-4 sp, sc in same ch sp, sc in each ch-2 sp around with 3 sc in each corner ch-4 sp, sc in same corner ch sp as beg sc, join in beg sc.

Rnd 3: **Ch 2** (*see Pattern Notes*), hdc in same st, sk next 2 sts, [(sl st, ch 2, hdc) in next st, sk next 2 sts] around, join in joining sl st of last rnd. Fasten off.

BEAR
HEAD
Rnd 1: Beg at snout, with warm brown, ch 2, 6 sc in 2nd ch from hook, **do not join** (*see Pattern Notes*). (*6 sc*)

Rnd 2: 2 sc in each st around. (*12 sc*)

Rnd 3: [Sc in each of next 2 sts, 2 sc in next st] around. *(16 sc)*

Rnd 4: Sc in each st around.

Rnd 5: [Sc in each of next 3 sts, 2 sc in next st] around. *(20 sc)*

Rnd 6: [Sc in each of next 4 sts, 2 sc in next st] around. *(24 sc)*

Rnd 7: [2 sc in next st, sc in each of next 5 sts] around. *(28 sc)*

Rnd 8: [Sc in each of next 6 sts, 2 sc in next st] around. *(32 sc)*

Rnd 9: Sc in each of first 12 sts, [sc in next st, 2 sc in next st] 4 times, sc in each of last 12 sts. *(36 sc)*

Rnd 10: Sc in each of first 12 sts, [sc in next st, 2 sc in next st] 6 times, sc in each of last 12 sts. *(42 sc)*

Rnd 11: [Sc in each of next 6 sts, 2 sc in next st] around. *(48 sc)*

Rnd 12: [2 sc in next st, sc in each of next 7 sts] around. *(54 sc)*

Rnd 13: [Sc in each of next 8 sts, 2 sc in next st] around. *(60 sc)*

Rnds 14–25: Sc in each st around.

Rnd 26: [Sc in each of next 8 sts, **sc dec** *(see Stitch Guide)* in next 2 sts] around. *(54 sc)*

Rnd 27: [Sc in each of next 7 sts, sc dec in next 2 sts] around. Stuff Head. *(48 sc)*

Rnd 28: [Sc in each of next 4 sts, sc dec in next 2 sts] around. *(40 sc)*

Rnd 29: [Sc in each of next 3 sts, sc dec in next 2 sts] around. *(32 sc)*

Rnds 30 & 31: [Sc in each of next 2 sts, sc dec in next 2 sts] around. *(18 sc at end of last rnd)*

Rnd 32: [Sc in next st, sc dec in next 2 sts] around. Finish stuffing Head. *(12 sc)*

Rnd 33: [Sc dec in next 2 sts] around, join with sl st in beg sc. Leaving long end, fasten off.

Weave long end through top of sts on last rnd, pull to close. Secure end.

FACIAL FEATURES
Using **satin stitch** *(see Fig. 1)*, with black, embroider eyes above snout over rnds 9–11 on Head, 1½ inches apart as shown in photo.

Fig. 1
Satin Stitch

Using satin stitch, with black, embroider nose over top section of rnds 2–6 in triangle below eyes as shown in photo.

Using **straight stitch** *(see Fig. 2)*, with black, embroider mouth below nose as shown in photo.

Fig. 2
Straight Stitch

EAR
MAKE 2.
Rnd 1: With warm brown, ch 2, 6 sc in 2nd ch from hook, **do not join.** *(6 sc)*

Row 2: 2 sc in each st around, **turn.** *(12 sc)*

Row 3: Ch 1, sc in first st, hdc in each of next 2 sts, 2 hdc in next st, 3 hdc in each of next 2 sts, 2 hdc in next st, hdc in each of next 2 sts, sc in next st, leaving last 2 sts unworked. Leaving long end, fasten off.

BODY
SHIRT
Rnd 1: Beg at neck, with white, ch 24, sc in first ch to form ring, sc in each ch around, join in beg sc. *(24 sc)*

Rnd 2: [Sc in next st, 2 sc in next st] around, **changing colors** *(see Stitch Guide)* to cherry red in last st, join in beg sc. Drop white, **do not fasten off**. *(36 sc)*

Rnd 3: Ch 1, sc in each of first 3 sts, 2 sc in next st, [sc in each of next 3 sts, 2 sc in next st] around, join in beg sc. *(45 sc)*

Rnd 4: Ch 1, sc in each st around, changing to white in last st, join in beg sc. Drop cherry red, **do not fasten off**.

Rnd 5: Ch 1, sc in each of first 4 sts, 2 sc in next st, [sc in each of next 4 sts, 2 sc in next st] around, join in beg sc. *(54 sc)*

Rnd 6: Ch 1, sc in each st around, changing to cherry red in last st, join in beg sc.

Rnd 7: Ch 1, sc in each of first 8 sts, 2 sc in next st, [sc in each of next 8 sts, 2 sc in next st] around, join in beg sc. *(60 sc)*

Rnd 8: Rep rnd 4.

Rnd 9: Ch 1, sc in each st around, join in beg sc.

Rnd 10: Rep rnd 6.

Rnd 11: Ch 1, sc in each st around, join in beg sc.

Rnd 12: Rep rnd 4.

Rnds 13–16: Rep rnds 9–12. At end of rnd 14, fasten off white. At end of last rnd, fasten off cherry red.

PANTS
Rnd 17: Working in **back lps** *(see Stitch Guide)*, join royal with sc in first st, sc in each st around, **do not join**.

Rnds 18–34: Sc in each st around.

Rnd 35: [Sc in each of next 4 sts, sc dec in next 2 sts] around. *(50 sc)*

Rnd 36: [Sc in each of next 3 sts, sc dec in next 2 sts] around. Stuff Body. *(40 sc)*

Rnd 37: [Sc in each of next 2 sts, sc dec in next 2 sts] around. *(30 sc)*

Rnd 38: [Sc in each of next 3 sts, sc dec in next 2 sts] around. *(24 sc)*

Rnd 39: [Sc in each of next 2 sts, sc dec in next 2 sts] around. *(18 sc)*

Rnd 40: [Sc in next st, sc dec in next 2 sts] around. Finish stuffing Body. *(12 sc)*

Rnd 41: [Sc dec in next 2 sts] around, join in beg sc. Leaving long end, fasten off. *(6 sc)*

Weave long end through top of sts of last rnd, pull to close. Secure end.

Sew Head to Body.

ARM
MAKE 2.
Rnd 1: With white, ch 20, sc in first ch to form ring, sc in each ch around, join in beg sc. *(20 sc)*

Rnd 2: Ch 1, sc in each st around, changing to cherry red in last st, join in beg sc. **Do not fasten off** white.

Rnd 3: Ch 1, sc in each st around, join in beg sc.

Rnd 4: Ch 1, sc in each st around, changing to white in last st, join in beg sc. **Do not fasten off** cherry red.

Rnd 5: Ch 1, sc in each st around, join in beg sc.

Rnd 6: Ch 1, sc in each st around, changing to cherry red in last st, join in beg sc.

Rnds 7–26: [Rep rnds 3–6 consecutively] 5 times. At end of last rnd, fasten off white.

Rnds 27 & 28: Rep rnds 3 and 4. At end of last rnd, fasten off.

LEFT HAND
Rnd 1: Working in back lps, join warm brown with sc in first st on 1 Arm, sc in each of next 2 sts, [2 sc in next st, sc in next st] 4 times, sc in each of last 9 sts, **do not join.** *(24 sc)*

Rnds 2–6: Sc in each st around.

Rnd 7: [Sc in each of next 2 sts, sc dec in next 2 sts] around. *(18 sc)*

Rnd 8: [Sc in next st, sc dec in next 2 sts] around. *(12 sc)*

Rnd 9: [Sc dec in next 2 sts] around, join in beg sc. Leaving long end, fasten off.

Weave long end through tops of sts on last rnd, pull to close. Secure end.

RIGHT HAND
Rnd 1: Working in back lps, join with sc in 11th st after joining on last rnd on rem Arm, sc in each of next 2 sts, [2 sc in next st, sc in next st] 4 times, sc in each of last 9 sts, do not join. *(24 sc)*

Rnds 2–9: Rep rnds 2–9 of Left Hand.

LEG
MAKE 2.
Rnd 1: Beg at top, with royal, ch 20, sc in first ch to form ring, sc in each ch around, **do not join.** *(20 sc)*

Rnds 2–28: Sc in each st around. At end of last rnd, join with sl st in beg sc. Fasten off.

FEET
Work same as for Hands.

PANT CUFF
MAKE 2.
With white, ch 25, sc in 2nd ch from hook, sc in next ch, changing to cherry red, *carry unused color behind work, sc in each of next 2 chs **, changing to white in last sc, sc in each of next 2 chs, changing to cherry red in last sc, rep from * across, ending last rep at **. Fasten off.

Sew Pant Cuff to last row of Pants as shown in photo.

Sew Arms and Legs to Body as shown in photo.

With sewing thread, sew 2-inch piece of hook-and-loop fastener to outer right Hand and right Foot, and to inner left Hand and left Foot.

COLLAR
With white, ch 33, 3 dc in 4th ch from hook, dc in each of next 28 chs, (3 dc, ch 2, sl st) in last ch. Fasten off.

Place Collar around neck with ends at center front. Sew in place.

HAT
CROWN

Row 1: With white, ch 13, sc in 2nd ch from hook and in each ch across, turn. *(12 sc)*

Row 2: Ch 1, sc in each st across, changing to cherry red in last st, turn. **Do not fasten off** white.

Row 3: Ch 1, sc in each st across, turn.

Row 4: Ch 1, sc in each st across, changing to white in last st, turn. **Do not fasten off** cherry red.

Row 5: Ch 1, sc in each st across, turn.

Row 6: Ch 1, sc in each st across, changing to cherry red in last st, turn.

Rows 7–54: [Rep rows 3–6 consecutively] 12 times.

Rows 55 & 56: Rep rows 3 and 4. At end of last row, fasten off cherry red.

Row 57: Working in starting ch on opposite side of row 1 and in back lps of sts on last row, fold piece in half, working through both thicknesses, ch 1, sl st in each st across, forming tube, **do not turn.**

Rnd 58: Working in ends of rows, sc in each row around, join in beg sc. Fasten off. *(56 sc)*

HAT BAND

Rnd 1: Working in back lps, join royal with sc in any st, sc in each st around, join in beg sc.

Rnd 2: Ch 1, sc in each st around, join in beg sc. Fasten off.

Rnd 3: Working in back lps, join white with sc in first st, sc in each of next 25 sts, sc dec in next 2 sts, sc in each of next 26 sts, sc dec in last 2 sts, join in beg sc. *(54 sc)*

BRIM

Rnd 4: Ch 1 *(does not count as first hdc)*, hdc in each of first 2 sts, 2 hdc in next st, [hdc in each of next 2 sts, 2 hdc in next st] around, join in beg hdc. *(72 hdc)*

Rnd 5: Ch 1, hdc in first st and in each st around, join in beg hdc.

Rnd 6: Ch 1, hdc in each of first 5 sts, 2 hdc in next st, [hdc in each of next 5 sts, 2 hdc in next st] around, join in beg hdc. Fasten off. *(84 hdc)*

HAT TOP

Rnd 1: With white, ch 2, 8 sc in 2nd ch from hook, **do not join.** *(8 sc)*

Rnd 2: 2 sc in each st around. *(16 sc)*

Rnd 3: [Sc in next st, 2 sc in next st] around. *(24 sc)*

Rnd 4: [Sc in each of next 2 sts, 2 sc in next st] around. *(32 sc)*

Rnd 5: [2 sc in next st, sc in each of next 3 sts] around. *(40 sc)*

Rnd 6: [Sc in each of next 4 sts, 2 sc in next st] around. *(48 sc)*

Rnd 7: [2 sc in next st, sc in each of next 5 sts] around, sl st in beg sc. Leaving long end, fasten off. *(56 sc)*

Using long end, sew Hat Top to ends of rows on Crown.

Stuff Hat and sew to top of Head as shown in photo.

Sew Ears slanted to rnds 3–5 of Brim in front as shown in photo. ∎

Bunny

SKILL LEVEL

■■■□
INTERMEDIATE

FINISHED SIZE
16 inches tall sitting, excluding Ears

MATERIALS
- Red Heart Super Saver medium (worsted) weight yarn (7 oz/ 364 yds/198g per skein):
  - 2 skeins #311 white
  - 3 oz/150yds/85g #373 petal pink
  - 1 oz/50 yds/28g #672 spring green
  - ½ oz/25 yds/14g each #312 black, #322 pale yellow, #530 orchid, #724 baby pink and #381 light blue
- Red Heart Classic medium (worsted) weight yarn (3½ oz/190 yds/99g per skein):
  - ½ oz/25 yds/14g #681 mist green
- Aunt Lydia's Classic size 10 crochet cotton (350 yds per ball):
  - 1 ball #401 orchid pink
- Size 7/1.65mm steel crochet hook
- Size H/8/5mm crochet hook or size needed to obtain gauge
- Tapestry needle
- Sewing needle
- Sewing thread
- 30 x 40-inch piece of pink flannel or blanket fabric
- Fiberfill
- 4-inch piece of hook-and-loop fastener
- Stitch marker

GAUGE
Size H hook and yarn: 4 sc = 1 inch

PATTERN NOTES
Use size H hook with yarn and size 7 hook with crochet cotton.

Join with slip stitch as indicated unless otherwise stated.

Work in continuous rounds, do not turn or join unless otherwise stated.

Mark first stitch of each round.

SPECIAL STITCH
Picot: Ch 3, sl st in side of last st worked.

INSTRUCTIONS
BLANKET
Rnd 1: Working around outer edge of fabric, using **size 7 hook** (*see Pattern Notes*), pushing hook through fabric ¼ inch from edge of fabric and with sts ¼ inch apart, join crochet cotton with sc near 1 corner, *evenly sp (ch 2, sc) across until you have even number of ch sps along side to next corner, ch 4 for corner, rep from * around, **join** (*see Pattern Notes*) in beg sc. Fasten off.

Rnd 2: Join petal pink with sc in any corner ch sp, sc in same ch sp, sc in each ch sp around with 3 sc in each corner ch sp, sc in same ch sp as beg sc, join in beg sc.

Rnd 3: Ch 1, sc in first st, *picot (*see Special Stitch*), sk next st**, sc in next st, rep from * around, ending last rep at **, join in beg sc. Fasten off.

BUNNY
HEAD
Rnd 1: Beg at top, with white, ch 2, 6 sc in 2nd ch from hook, **do not join** (*see Pattern Notes*). (*6 sc*)

Rnd 2: 2 sc in each st around. (*12 sc*)

Rnd 3: [Sc in next st, 2 sc in next st] around. (*18 sc*)

Rnd 4: [Sc in each of next 2 sts, 2 sc in next st] around. (*24 sc*)

Rnd 5: [2 sc in next st, sc in each of next 3 sts] around. *(30 sc)*

Rnd 6: [Sc in each of next 4 sts, 2 sc in next st] around. *(36 sc)*

Rnd 7: [Sc in each of next 5 sts, 2 sc in next st] around. *(42 sc)*

Rnd 8: Sc in each st around.

Rnd 9: [Sc in each of next 6 sts, 2 sc in next st] around. *(48 sc)*

Rnd 10: Sc in each st around.

Rnd 11: [Sc in each of next 11 sts, 2 sc in next st] around. *(52 sc)*

Rnds 12–26: Sc in each st around.

Rnd 27: [Sc in each of next 11 sts, **sc dec** *(see Stitch Guide)* in next 2 sts] around. Stuff Head. *(48 sc)*

Rnd 28: [Sc in each of next 4 sts, sc dec in next 2 sts] around. *(40 sc)*

Rnd 29: [Sc in each of next 3 sts, sc dec in next 2 sts] around. Finish stuffing Head. *(32 sc)*

Rnd 30: [Sc in each of next 2 sts, sc dec in next 2 sts] around, join in beg sc. Leaving long end, fasten off. *(24 sc)*

CHEEK
MAKE 2.

Rnds 1–4: Rep rnds 1–4 of Head. *(24 sc at end of last rnd)*

Rnds 5–7: Sc in each st around. At end of last rnd, leaving long end, fasten off.

Stuff Cheeks.

Using long end, sew Cheeks side by side to rnds 18–27 on Head as shown in photo.

NOSE

Rnd 1: With petal pink, ch 2, 5 sc in 2nd ch from hook, **do not join**. *(5 sc)*

Rnd 2: 2 sc in each st around. *(10 sc)*

Rnd 3: Sc in each st around. Stuff Nose.

Rnd 4: [Sc dec in next 2 sts] around, join in beg sc. Leaving long end, fasten off. *(5 sc)*

Sew Nose to Head between Cheeks as shown in photo.

Using **satin stitch** *(see Fig. 1)*, with black, embroider eyes on Head above Nose and Cheeks 1¾ inches apart.

Fig. 1
Satin Stitch

EAR
INNER EAR
MAKE 2.

Row 1: With petal pink, ch 17, sc in 2nd ch from hook and in each of next 5 chs, hdc in each of next 5 chs, dc in each of next 4 chs, 3 dc in last ch, working on opposite side of ch, 3 dc in next ch, dc in each of next 4 chs, hdc in each of next 5 chs, sc in each of last 6 chs, turn. *(36 sts)*

Row 2: Ch 1, sc in each of first 11 sts, hdc in each of next 5 sts, 2 hdc in each of next 4 sts, hdc in each of next 5 sts, sc in each of last 11 sts. Fasten off. *(40 sts)*

OUTER EAR
MAKE 2.

Row 1: With white, ch 17, sc in 2nd ch from hook and in each of next 5 chs, hdc in each of next 5 chs, dc in each of next 4 chs, 3 dc in last ch, working on opposite side of ch, 3 dc in next ch, dc in each of next 4 chs, hdc in each of next 5 chs, sc in each of last 6 chs, turn. *(36 sts)*

Row 2: Ch 1, sc in each of first 11 sts, hdc in each of next 5 sts, 2 hdc in each of next 4 sts, hdc in each of next 5 sts, sc in each of last 11 sts, turn. *(40 sts)*

Row 3: Place 1 Inner Ear on top of Outer Ear WS tog, working through both thicknesses and in **back lps** *(see Stitch Guide)* on Inner Ear and both lps on Outer Ear, ch 1, sc in each of first 18 sts, 2 sc in each of next 4 sts, sc in each of last 18 sts. Leaving long end, fasten off.

Using long end, sew Ears to top of Head 1½ inches apart as shown in photo.

BODY

Rnd 1: Beg at neck, with white, ch 24, sc in first ch to form ring, sc in each ch around, do not join. *(24 sc)*

Rnd 2: [Sc in next st, 2 sc in next st] around. *(36 sc)*

Rnd 3: [Sc in each of next 3 sts, 2 sc in next st] around. *(45 sc)*

Rnd 4: Sc in each st around.

Rnd 5: [Sc in each of next 4 sts, 2 sc in next st] around. *(54 sc)*

Rnd 6: Sc in each st around.

Rnd 7: [Sc in each of next 8 sts, 2 sc in next st] around. *(60 sc)*

Rnds 8–34: Sc in each st around.

Rnd 35: [Sc in each of next 4 sts, sc dec in next 2 sts] around. *(50 sc)*

Rnd 36: [Sc in each of next 3 sts, sc dec in next 2 sts] around. Stuff Body. *(40 sc)*

Rnd 37: [Sc in each of next 2 sts, sc dec in next 2 sts] around. *(30 sc)*

Rnd 38: [Sc in each of next 3 sts, sc dec in next 2 sts] around. *(24 sc)*

Rnd 39: [Sc in each of next 2 sts, sc dec in next 2 sts] around. *(18 sc)*

Rnd 40: [Sc in next st, sc dec in next 2 sts] around. Finish stuffing Body. *(12 sc)*

Rnd 41: [Sc dec in next 2 sts] around, join in beg sc. Leaving long end, fasten off. *(6 sc)*

Weave long end through top of sts of last rnd, pull to close. Secure end.

Using long end on Head, sew Head to Body.

ARM
MAKE 2.

Rnd 1: Beg at top, with white, ch 20, sc in first ch to form ring, sc in each ch around, **do not join.** *(20 sc)*

Rnds 2–28: Sc in each st around.

Rnd 29: Sc in each of first 3 sts, [2 sc in next st, sc in next st] 4 times, sc in each of last 9 sts. *(24 sc)*

Rnds 30–34: Sc in each st around.

Rnd 35: [Sc in each of next 2 sts, sc dec in next 2 sts] around. *(18 sc)*

Rnd 36: [Sc in next st, sc dec in next 2 sts] around. *(12 sc)*

Rnd 37: [Sc dec in next 2 sts] around. Leaving long end, fasten off. *(6 sc)*

Weave long end through top of sts on last rnd, pull to close. Secure end.

Stuff Arm lightly, leaving the top 2 inches unstuffed.

Flatten rnd 1 and sew closed.

Sew Arms to rnds 4–11 at sides of Body as shown in photo.

LEG
MAKE 2.
Rnds 1–37: Rep rnds 1–37 of Arm.

Weave long end through top of sts on last rnd, pull to close. Secure end.

Stuff Leg lightly, leaving the top 2 inches unstuffed.

Flatten rnd 1 and sew closed.

Sew Legs to sides of Body as shown in photo.

With sewing thread, sew 2-inch piece of hook-and-loop fastener to outer right Arm and right Foot, and to inner left Arm and left Foot.

TAIL
Rnds 1–4: Rep rnds 1–4 of Head. *(24 sc at end of last rnd)*

Rnds 5–7: Sc in each st around. At end of last rnd, leaving long end, fasten off.

Stuff Tail.

Sew to center bottom back of Body.

BASKET
Rnd 1: Beg at bottom, with spring green, ch 8, sc in 2nd ch from hook, sc in each of next 5 chs, 3 sc in last ch, working on opposite side of ch, sc in each of next 6 chs, 3 sc in last ch, *do not join. (18 sc)*

Rnd 2: [Sc in each of next 6 sts, 2 sc in each of next 3 sts] around. *(24 sc)*

Rnd 3: *Sc in each of next 6 sts, [sc in next st, 2 sc in next st] 3 times, rep from * once. *(30 sc)*

Rnd 4: *Sc in each of next 6 sts, [sc in each of next 2 sts, 2 sc in next st] 3 times, rep from * once. *(36 sc)*

Rnd 5: *Sc in each of next 9 sts, [2 sc in next st, sc in each of next 2 sts] 3 times, rep from * once, join in beg sc. *(42 sc)*

Rnd 6: Working in back lps, ch 1, hdc in first st and in each st around, join in beg hdc.

Rnds 7–10: Ch 1, hdc in first st and in each st around, join in beg hdc. At end of last rnd, fasten off.

TRIM
Rnd 1: Join white with sc in 4th st before joining, sc in each st around, join in beg sc, **turn.**

Rnd 2: Working in back lps, ch 3, 4 dc in same st, *ch 1, sk next 2 sts, sc in next st, ch 1, sk next 2 sts**, 5 dc in next st, rep from * around, ending last rep at **, join in 3rd ch of beg ch-3. Fasten off.

HANDLE
With white, ch 32, sl st in 2nd ch from hook, [ch 1, sk next ch, sl st in next ch] across. Fasten off.

Sew ends to row 1 of Trim at sides of Basket.

EGG
MAKE 4 USING MIST GREEN, PALE YELLOW, ORCHID, LIGHT BLUE AND BABY PINK.
Rnd 1: Ch 2, 6 sc in 2nd ch from hook, **do not join.** *(6 sc)*

Rnd 2: 2 sc in each st around. *(12 sc)*

Rnd 3: [Sc in each of next 3 sts, 2 sc in next st] around. *(15 sc)*

Rnd 4: [Sc in each of next 4 sts, 2 sc in next st] around, join in beg sc. Fasten off. *(18 sc)*

Rnd 5: Working in back lps, join 2nd color with sc in first st, **changing colors** (*see Stitch Guide*) to 3rd color, *sc in next st, changing to 2nd color**, sc in next st, changing to 3rd color, rep from * around, ending last rep at **, join in beg sc.

Rnd 6: Ch 1, sc in first st, changing to 3rd color, sc in each of next 2 sts, changing to 2nd color, [sc in next st, changing to 3rd color, sc in each of next 2 sts, changing to 2nd color in last st] around, join in beg sc. Fasten off both colors.

Rnd 7: Working in back lps, join first color with sc in any st, sc in each st around, **do not join**. Stuff Egg.

Rnd 8: [Sc in next st, sc dec in next 2 sts] around. (*12 sc*)

Rnd 9: [Sc dec in next 2 sts] around, join in beg sc. Leaving long end, fasten off.

Finish stuffing Egg.

Weave long end through top of sts on last rnd, pull to close. Secure end.

Tack Eggs tog and place in Basket.

Place Basket on 1 Arm as shown in photo on page 15. ■

Penguin

SKILL LEVEL
INTERMEDIATE

FINISHED SIZE
16 inches tall sitting

MATERIALS
- Red Heart Super Saver Economy medium (worsted) weight yarn (7 oz/364 yds/198g):
  2 skeins #312 black
  1 skein #381 light blue
  1 oz/50 yds/28g #316 soft white
- Red Heart Super Saver Regular medium (worsted) weight yarn (3 oz/160 yds/85g per skein):
  1 oz/50 yds/28g #354 vibrant orange
- Aunt Lydia's Classic size 10 crochet cotton (350 yds per ball):
  1 ball #480 delft
- Size 7/1.65mm steel crochet hook
- Size H/8/5mm crochet hook or size needed to obtain gauge
- Tapestry needle
- Sewing needle
- Sewing thread
- 30 x 40 inch-piece of penguin print flannel or blanket fabric
- Fiberfill
- 4-inch piece of hook-and-loop fastener
- Pompom maker
- Stitch marker

4 MEDIUM

GAUGE
Size H hook and yarn: 4 sc = 1 inch

PATTERN NOTES
Use size H hook with yarn and size 7 hook with crochet cotton.

Join with slip stitch as indicated unless otherwise stated.

Chain-3 at beginning of row or round counts as first double crochet unless otherwise stated.

Work in continuous rounds, do not turn or join unless otherwise stated.

Mark first stitch of each round.

SPECIAL STITCH
Split cluster (split cl): Holding back last lp of each st on hook, 2 dc in each place indicated, yo, pull through all lps on hook.

INSTRUCTIONS
BLANKET
Rnd 1: Working around outer edge of fabric, using **size 7 hook** (*see Pattern Notes*), pushing hook through fabric ¼ inch from edge of fabric and with sts ¼ inch apart, join crochet cotton with sc near 1 corner, *evenly sp (ch 2, sc) across until you have an even number of ch sps along side to next corner, ch 4 for corner, rep from * around, **join** (*see Pattern Notes*) in beg sc. Fasten off.

Rnd 2: Join light blue with sc in any corner ch sp, sc in same ch sp, sc in each ch-2 sp around with 3 sc in each corner ch-4 sp, sc in same ch sp as beg sc, join in beg sc.

Rnd 3: Ch 3 (*see Pattern Notes*), 4 dc in same st, sk next 2 sts, sl st in next st, sk next st, [5 dc in next st, sk next 2 sts, sl st in next st, sk next st] around, join in 3rd ch of beg ch-3. Fasten off.

PENGUIN
HEAD
Rnd 1: Beg at top, with black, ch 2, 6 sc in 2nd ch from hook, **do not join** (*see Pattern Notes*). (*6 sc*)

Rnd 2: 2 sc in each st around. *(12 sc)*

Rnd 3: [Sc in next st, 2 sc in next st] around. *(18 sc)*

Rnd 4: [Sc in each of next 2 sts, 2 sc in next st] around. *(24 sc)*

Rnd 5: [2 sc in next st, sc in each of next 3 sts] around. *(30 sc)*

Rnd 6: [Sc in each of next 4 sts, 2 sc in next st] around. *(36 sc)*

Rnd 7: [Sc in each of next 5 sts, 2 sc in next st] around. *(42 sc)*

Rnd 8: Sc in each st around.

Rnd 9: [Sc in each of next 6 sts, 2 sc in next st] around. *(48 sc)*

Rnd 10: Sc in each st around.

Rnd 11: [Sc in each of next 11 sts, 2 sc in next st] around. *(52 sc)*

Rnds 12–24: Sc in each st around.

Rnd 25: [Sc in each of next 11 sts, **sc dec** *(see Stitch Guide)* in next 2 sts] around. Stuff Head. *(48 sc)*

Rnd 26: [Sc in each of next 4 sts, sc dec in next 2 sts] around. *(40 sc)*

Rnd 27: [Sc in each of next 3 sts, sc dec in next 2 sts] around. Finish stuffing Head. *(32 sc)*

Rnd 28: [Sc in each of next 2 sts, sc dec in next 2 sts] around, join in beg sc. Leaving long end, fasten off. *(24 sc)*

BODY
Rnd 1: Beg at neck, with black, ch 24, sc in first ch to form ring, sc in each ch around, do not join. *(24 sc)*

Rnd 2: [Sc in next st, 2 sc in next st] around. *(36 sc)*

Rnd 3: [Sc in each of next 3 sts, 2 sc in next st] around. *(45 sc)*

Rnd 4: Sc in each st around.

Rnd 5: [Sc in each of next 4 sts, 2 sc in next st] around. *(54 sc)*

Rnd 6: Sc in each st around.

Rnd 7: [Sc in each of next 8 sts, 2 sc in next st] around. *(60 sc)*

Rnds 8–34: Sc in each st around.

Rnd 35: [Sc in each of next 4 sts, sc dec in next 2 sts] around. *(50 sc)*

Rnd 36: [Sc in each of next 3 sts, sc dec in next 2 sts] around. Stuff Body. *(40 sc)*

Rnd 37: [Sc in each of next 2 sts, sc dec in next 2 sts] around. *(30 sc)*

Rnd 38: [Sc in each of next 3 sts, sc dec in next 2 sts] around. *(24 sc)*

Rnd 39: [Sc in each of next 2 sts, sc dec in next 2 sts] around. *(18 sc)*

Rnd 40: [Sc in next st, sc dec in next 2 sts] around. Finish stuffing Body. *(12 sc)*

Rnd 41: [Sc dec in next 2 sts] around, join in beg sc. Leaving long end, fasten off. *(6 sc)*

Weave long end through top of sts of last rnd, pull to close. Secure end.

Using long end on Head, sew Head to top of Body.

FACE PANEL
Row 1: Beg at bottom or neck edge, with soft white, ch 13, sc in 2nd ch from hook and in each ch across, turn. *(12 sc)*

Rows 2–5: Ch 1, 2 sc in first st, sc in each st across with 2 sc in last st, turn. *(20 sc at end of last row)*

Rows 6–8: Ch 1, sc in each st across, turn.

Rows 9–11: Ch 1, sc in first st, sc dec in next 2 sts, sc in each st across to last 3 sts, sc dec in next 2 sts, sc in last st, turn. *(14 sc at end of last row)*

Rows 12–15: Ch 1, sc in each st across, turn.

Rows 16 & 17: Rep row 9. *(10 sc at end of last row)*

Row 18: Ch 1, (sc, hdc) in first st, hdc in each of next 2 sts, sc in next st, sl st in each of next 2 sts, sc in next st, hdc in each of next 2 sts, (hdc, sc, sl st) in last st. Fasten off.

EDGING
Working around outer edge in ends of rows, in sts and in starting ch on opposite side of row 1, join soft white with sc in row 1, evenly sp 17 sc in ends of rows across, working in sts on row 18, 2 sc in each of first 2 sts, hdc in each of next 2 sts, sc in next st, sl st in each of next 2 sts, sc in next st, hdc in each of next 2 sts, 2 sc in each of last 2 sts, evenly sp 18 sc in ends of rows across, ch 1, sc in each ch across, ch 1, join in beg sc. Fasten off.

BODY PANEL
Row 1: Beg at bottom of neck edge, with soft white, ch 13, sc in 2nd ch from hook and in each ch across, turn. *(12 sc)*

Row 2: Ch 1, sc in each st across, turn.

Rows 3 & 4: Ch 1, 2 sc in first st, sc in each st across with 2 sc in last st, turn. *(16 sc at end of last row)*

Rows 5–7: Ch 1, sc in each st across, turn.

Row 8: Rep row 3. *(18 sc)*

Row 9: Ch 1, sc in each st across, turn.

Row 10: Rep row 3. *(20 sc)*

Rows 11–32: Ch 1, sc in each st across, turn.

Row 33: Ch 1, sc in first st, sc dec in next 2 sts, sc in each st across to last 3 sts, sc dec in next 2 sts, sc in last st, turn. *(18 sc)*

Row 34: Ch 1, sc in first st, sc dec in next 2 sts, sc in each st across to last 3 sts, sc dec in next 2 sts, sc in last st. Fasten off. *(16 sc)*

EDGING
Working around outer edge in ends of rows, in sts and in starting ch on opposite side of row 1, join soft white with sc in row 1, evenly sp 33 sc in ends of rows across, working in sts on row 18, 2 sc in first st, sc in each st across with 2 sc in last st, evenly sp 34 sc in ends of rows across, ch 1, sc in each ch across, ch 1, join in beg sc. Fasten off.

Sew Face Panel to Head as shown in photo and sew Body Panel to front of Body.

BEAK
Row 1: With vibrant orange, ch 3, sc in 2nd ch from hook, sc in last ch, turn. *(2 sc)*

Rows 2–4: Ch 1, 2 sc in first st, sc in each st across with 2 sc in last st, turn. *(8 sc at end of last row)*

Row 5: Ch 1, sc in each st across, turn.

Row 6: Working in **front lps** (*see Stitch Guide*), ch 1, sc in each st across, turn.

Row 7: Ch 1, sc in first st, sc dec in next 2 sts, sc in each st across to last 3 sts, sc dec in next 2 sts, sc in last st, turn. (*6 sc*)

Row 8: Ch 1, sc in first st, [sc dec in next 2 sts] twice, sc in last st, turn. (*4 sc*)

Row 9: Ch 1, [sc dec in next 2 sts] twice, turn. (*2 sc*)

Row 10: Ch 1, sc in each st across. Fasten off.

EDGING
Join vibrant orange with sc in end of row 6, sc in each of next 4 rows, 2 sc in each of next 2 sts on row 10, sc in end of each row across, 2 sc in each of next 2 chs on opposite side of row 1, sc in end of each row across, join in beg sc. Fasten off.

Fold Beak along row 6. Sew fold to center of row 9 on Face Panel as shown in photo.

Using **satin stitch** (*see Fig. 1*), with black, embroider eyes above Beak 1 inch apart as shown in photo.

Fig. 1
Satin Stitch

ARM
MAKE 2.

Rnd 1: Beg at top, with black, ch 20, sc in first ch to form ring, sc in each ch around, **do not join**. (*20 sc*)

Rnds 2–28: Sc in each st around.

Rnd 29: [Sc in each of next 4 sts, 2 sc in next st] around. (*24 sc*)

Rnd 30: Sc in each of first 11 sts, 2 sc in each of next 2 sts, sc in each of last 11 sts. (*26 sc*)

Rnd 31: Sc in each of next 11 sts, [**split cl** (*see Special Stitch*) in next 2 sts] twice, sc in each of last 11 sts.

Rnd 32: Sc in each of first 11 sts, sk next 2 split cls, sc in each of last 11 sts. (*22 sc*)

Rnd 33: Sc in each of first 3 sts, *sc dec in next 2 sts**, sc in each of next 3 sts, rep from * across, ending last rep at **, sc in each of last 2 sts. (*18 sc*)

Rnd 34: Sc in each of first 7 sts, [split cl in next 2 sts] twice, sc in each of last 7 sts. (*16 sc*)

Rnd 35: Sc in each of first 7 sts, sk next 2 split cls, sc in each of last 7 sts. (*14 sc*)

Rnd 36: Sc in first st, *sc dec in next 2 sts, sc in each of next 2 sts, sc dec in next 2 sts*, sc in next st, rep between * once. (*10 sc*)

Rnd 37: Sc in each of first 3 sts, [split cl in next 2 sts] twice, sc in each of last 3 sts. (*8 sts*)

Rnd 38: [Sk next st, sl st in next st] around, join in beg sl st. Leaving long end, fasten off.

Weave long end through top of sts on last rnd, pull to close. Secure end.

Stuff Arm, leaving top 2 inches unstuffed.

Flatten rnd 1 and sew closed. Sew to sides of Body as shown in photo.

LEG
MAKE 2.

Rnd 1: Beg at top, with black, ch 20, sc in first ch to form ring, sc in each ch around, **do not join**. (*20 sc*)

Rnds 2–28: Sc in each st around. At end of last rnd, fasten off.

Rnd 29: Join vibrant orange with sc in first st, sc in each of next 3 sts, 2 sc in next st, [sc in each of next 4 sts, 2 sc in next st] around. (*24 sc*)

Rnds 30–34: Sc in each st around.

Rnd 35: Sl st in next st, ch 3, dc in same st, 2 dc in each of next 2 sts, sl st in next st, [2 dc in each of next 3 sts, sl st in next st] around, join in beg sl st. Leaving long end, fasten off.

Flatten last rnd and working in **back lps** (see *Stitch Guide*), sew closed.

Stuff Leg, leaving top 2 inches unstuffed.

Flatten rnd 1 and sew closed. Sew Legs to sides of Body as shown in photo.

With sewing thread, sew 2-inch piece of hook- and-loop fastener to outer right Hand and right Foot, and to inner left Hand and left Foot.

HAT
RIBBING
Row 1: With light blue, ch 7, sc in 2nd ch from hook and in each ch across, turn. (*6 sc*)

Rows 2–48: Working in back lps, ch 1, sc in each st across, turn.

Row 49: Holding row 1 and row 48 tog, working in starting ch of opposite side of row 1 and back lps of sts on row 48 at same time, ch 1, sc in each st across, do not turn.

CROWN
Rnd 1: Working in ends of rows of Ribbing, ch 1, evenly sp 48 sc around, join in beg sc. (*48 sc*)

Rnds 2–6: Ch 1, sc in each st around, join in beg sc.

Rnd 7: Ch 1, sc in each of first 4 sts, sc dec in next 2 sts, [sc in each of next 4 sts, sc dec in next 2 sts] around, join in beg sc. (*40 sc*)

Rnds 8 & 9: Rep rnd 2.

Rnd 10: Ch 1, sc in each of first 3 sts, sc dec in next 2 sts, [sc in each of next 3 sts, sc dec in next 2 sts] around, join in beg sc. (*32 sc*)

Rnds 11 & 12: Rep rnd 2.

Rnd 13: Ch 1, sc in each of first 2 sts, sc dec in next 2 sts, [sc in each of next 2 sts, sc dec in next 2 sts] around, join in beg sc. (*24 sc*)

Rnds 14 & 15: Ch 1, sc dec in first 2 sts, [sc dec in next 2 sts] around, join in beg sc dec. At end of last rnd, leaving long end, fasten off. (*6 sc at end of last rnd*)

Weave long end through top of sts on last rnd, pull to close. Secure end.

POMPOM
Using light blue and pompom maker, make 2-inch pompom.

Attach Pompom to last rnd on Hat.

Place Hat on Head and sew in place as shown in photo.

SCARF
Row 1: With light blue, ch 5, sc in 2nd ch from hook and in each ch across, turn. (*4 sc*)

Rows 2–85: Ch 1, sc in each st across, turn.

Row 86: Ch 1, sc in each st across. Fasten off.

FRINGE
Cut 16 strands of light blue, each 5 inches in length. Holding 2 strands tog, fold in half, pull fold through st, pull ends through fold. Pull to tighten.

Attach Fringe in each st and ch across each short end of Scarf.

Tie Scarf around neck as shown in photo. ■

Snowman

SKILL LEVEL

INTERMEDIATE

FINISHED SIZE
16 inches tall sitting, including Hat

MATERIALS
- Red Heart Super Saver Economy medium (worsted) weight yarn (7 oz/364 yds/198g):
  1 skein #311 white
  3 oz/150yds/85g each #368 paddy green and #312 black
  1 oz/50 yds/28g #319 cherry red
- Red Heart Super Saver Regular medium (worsted) weight yarn (3 oz/160 yds/ 85g per skein):
  ½ oz/25 yds/14g #354 vibrant orange
- Aunt Lydia's Classic size 10 crochet cotton (350 yds per ball):
  1 ball #494 victory red
- Size 7/1.65mm steel crochet hook
- Size H/8/5mm crochet hook
  or size needed to obtain gauge
- Tapestry needle
- Sewing needle
- Sewing thread
- 30 x 40-inch piece of red flannel or blanket fabric
- Fiberfill
- 4-inch piece of hook-and-loop fastener
- Stitch marker

GAUGE
Size H hook and yarn: 4 sc = 1 inch

PATTERN NOTES
Use size H hook with yarn and size 7 hook with crochet cotton.

Join with slip stitch as indicated unless otherwise stated.

Work in continuous rounds, do not turn or join unless otherwise stated.

Mark first stitch of each round.

SPECIAL STITCH
Cluster (cl): Holding back last lp of each st on hook, 3 dc in place indicated, yo, pull through all lps on hook.

INSTRUCTIONS
BLANKET
Rnd 1: Working around outer edge of fabric, using **size 7 hook** (*see Pattern Notes*), pushing hook through fabric ¼ inch from edge of fabric and with sts ¼ inch apart, join crochet cotton with sc near 1 corner, *evenly sp (ch 2, sc) across until you have even number of ch sps along side to next corner, ch 4 for corner, rep from * around, **join** (*see Pattern Notes*) in beg sc. Fasten off.

Rnd 2: Join paddy green with sc in any corner ch sp, sc in same ch sp, sc in each ch sp around with 3 sc in each corner ch sp, sc in same ch sp as beg sc, join in beg sc.

Rnd 3: *Ch 4, sl st in 2nd ch from hook, sc in next ch, dc in next ch, sk next 2 sts**, sl st in each of next 2 sts, rep from * around, ending last rep at **, sl st in last st, join in joining sl st of last rnd. Fasten off.

SNOWMAN
HEAD
Rnd 1: Beg at top, with white, ch 2, 6 sc in 2nd ch from hook, **do not join** (*see Pattern Notes*). (*6 sc*)

Rnd 2: 2 sc in each st around. (*12 sc*)

Rnd 3: [Sc in next st, 2 sc in next st] around. (*18 sc*)

Rnd 4: [Sc in each of next 2 sts, 2 sc in next st] around. *(24 sc)*

Rnd 5: [2 sc in next st, sc in each of next 3 sts] around. *(30 sc)*

Rnd 6: [Sc in each of next 4 sts, 2 sc in next st] around. *(36 sc)*

Rnd 7: [Sc in each of next 5 sts, 2 sc in next st] around. *(42 sc)*

Rnd 8: Sc in each st around.

Rnd 9: [Sc in each of next 6 sts, 2 sc in next st] around. *(48 sc)*

Rnd 10: Sc in each st around.

Rnd 11: [Sc in each of next 11 sts, 2 sc in next st] around. *(52 sc)*

Rnds 12–23: Sc in each st around.

Rnd 24: [Sc in each of next 11 sts, **sc dec** *(see Stitch Guide)* in next 2 sts] around. Stuff Head. *(48 sc)*

Rnd 25: [Sc in each of next 4 sts, sc dec in next 2 sts] around. *(40 sc)*

Rnd 26: [Sc in each of next 3 sts, sc dec in next 2 sts] around. Finish stuffing Head. *(32 sc)*

Rnd 27: [Sc in each of next 2 sts, sc dec in next 2 sts] around, join in beg sc. Leaving long end, fasten off. *(24 sc)*

BODY

Rnd 1: Beg at neck, with white, ch 24, sc in first ch to form ring, sc in each ch around, do not join. *(24 sc)*

Rnd 2: [Sc in next st, 2 sc in next st] around. *(36 sc)*

Rnd 3: [Sc in each of next 3 sts, 2 sc in next st] around. *(45 sc)*

Rnd 4: Sc in each st around.

Rnd 5: [Sc in each of next 4 sts, 2 sc in next st] around. *(54 sc)*

Rnd 6: Sc in each st around.

Rnd 7: [Sc in each of next 8 sts, 2 sc in next st] around. *(60 sc)*

Rnds 8–34: Sc in each st around.

Rnd 35: [Sc in each of next 4 sts, sc dec in next 2 sts] around. *(50 sc)*

Rnd 36: [Sc in each of next 3 sts, sc dec in next 2 sts] around. Stuff Body. *(40 sc)*

Rnd 37: [Sc in each of next 2 sts, sc dec in next 2 sts] around. *(30 sc)*

Rnd 38: [Sc in each of next 3 sts, sc dec in next 2 sts] around. (*24 sc*)

Rnd 39: [Sc in each of next 2 sts, sc dec in next 2 sts] around. (*18 sc*)

Rnd 40: [Sc in next st, sc dec in next 2 sts] around. Finish stuffing Body. (*12 sc*)

Rnd 41: [Sc dec in next 2 sts] around, join in beg sc. Leaving long end, fasten off. (*6 sc*)

Weave long end through top of sts of last rnd, pull to close. Secure end.

BUTTON
MAKE 3.
With paddy green, ch 3, **cl** (*see Special Stitch*) in 3rd ch from hook, sl st in same ch. Fasten off.

Sew Buttons 1½ inches apart down front of Body.

NOSE
Rnd 1: With vibrant orange, ch 2, 6 sc in 2nd ch from hook, **do not join**. (*6 sc*)

Rnd 2: Sc in each st around.

Rnd 3: [Sc in each of next 2 sts, 2 sc in next st] around. (*8 sc*)

Rnd 4: Sc in each st around.

Rnd 5: [Sc in each of next 3 sts, 2 sc in next st] around. (*10 sc*)

Rnd 6: [2 sc in next st, sc in each of next 4 sts] around. (*12 sc*)

Rnd 7: Sc in each st around, join in beg sc. Leaving long end, fasten off.

Stuff Nose.

Using long end on Nose, sew Nose to Head over rnds 17–21.

Using **satin stitch** (*see Fig. 1*), with black, embroider eyes over rnds 14–17 on Head 2 inches apart above Nose as shown in photo.

Fig. 1
Satin Stitch

Using **straight stitch** (*see Fig. 2*), with black, embroider mouth below Nose as shown in photo.

Fig. 2
Straight Stitch

Using long end on Head, sew Head to Body.

ARM
MAKE 2.
Rnd 1: Beg at top, with white, ch 20, sc in first ch to form ring, sc in each ch around, **do not join**. (*20 sc*)

Rnds 2–28: Sc in each st around.

Rnd 29: Sc in each of first 3 sts, [2 sc in next st, sc in next st] 4 times, sc in each of last 9 sts. (*24 sc*)

Rnds 30–34: Sc in each st around.

Rnd 35: [Sc in each of next 2 sts, sc dec in next 2 sts] around. (*18 sc*)

Rnd 36: [Sc in next st, sc dec in next 2 sts] around. (*12 sc*)

Rnd 37: [Sc dec in next 2 sts] around. Leaving long end, fasten off. (*6 sc*)

Weave long end through top of sts on last rnd, pull to close. Secure end.

Stuff Arm lightly, leaving the top 2 inches unstuffed.

Flatten rnd 1 and sew closed.

Sew Arms to rnds 4–11 at sides of Body as shown in photo.

LEG
MAKE 2.
Rnds 1–27: Rep rnds 1–27 of Arm. At end of last rnd, join in beg sc. Fasten off.

FOOT
Rnd 28: Join black with sc in first st, sc in each st around, do not join.

Rnd 29: Sc in each of first 3 sts, [2 sc in next st, sc in next st] 4 times, sc in each of last 9 sts. (24 sc)

Rnds 30–34: Sc in each st around.

Rnd 35: [Sc in each of next 2 sts, sc dec in next 2 sts] around. (18 sc)

Rnd 36: [Sc in next st, sc dec in next 2 sts] around. (12 sc)

Rnd 37: [Sc dec in next 2 sts] around. Leaving long end, fasten off. (6 sc)

Weave long end through top of sts on last rnd, pull to close. Secure end.

Stuff Leg lightly, leaving the top 2 inches unstuffed.

Flatten rnd 1 and sew closed.

Sew Legs to sides of Body as shown in photo.

HAT
Rnd 1: Beg at top with black, ch 2, 6 sc in 2nd ch from hook, do not join. (6 sc)

Rnd 2: 2 sc in each st around. (12 sc)

Rnd 3: [Sc in next st, 2 sc in next st] around. (18 sc)

Rnd 4: [Sc in each of next 2 sts, 2 sc in next st] around. (24 sc)

Rnd 5: [2 sc in next st, sc in each of next 3 sts] around. (30 sc)

Rnd 6: [Sc in each of next 4 sts, 2 sc in next st] around. (36 sc)

Rnd 7: [Sc in each of next 5 sts, 2 sc in next st] around. (42 sc)

Rnd 8: [2 sc in next st, sc in each of next 6 sts] around. (48 sc)

Rnd 9: [Sc in each of next 5 sts, 2 sc in next st] around. (56 sc)

Rnds 10–19: Sc in each st around. At end of last rnd, join in beg sc. Fasten off.

Rnd 20: Working in **back lps** (see Stitch Guide), join cherry red with sc in first st, sc in each st around, join in beg sc.

Rnd 21: Working in both lps, ch 1, sc in each st around, join in beg sc. Fasten off.

Rnd 22: Working in back lps, join black in first sc, sc in each st around, join in beg sc.

BRIM
Rnd 23: Ch 1, sc in each of first 3 sts, 2 sc in next st, [sc in each of next 3 sts, 2 sc in next st] around, join in beg sc. (70 sc)

Rnd 24: Ch 1, sc in each of first 4 sts, 2 sc in next st, [sc in each of next 4 sts, 2 sc in next st] around, join in beg sc. (84 sc)

Rnds 25–27: Ch 1, sc in each st around, join in beg sc. At end of last rnd, fasten off.

Lightly stuff Hat. Sew to top of Head as shown in photo.

SCARF
Row 1: With cherry red, ch 5, sc in 2nd ch from hook and in each ch across, turn. (4 sc)

Row 2: Ch 1, sc in each st across, **changing colors** (see Stitch Guide) to paddy green in last st made, turn. **Do not fasten off red.**

Row 3: Ch 1, sc in each st across, turn.

Row 4: Ch 1, sc in each st across, changing to cherry red in last st made, turn. **Do not fasten off paddy green.**

Row 5: Ch 1, sc in each st across, turn.

Row 6: Ch 1, sc in each st across, changing to paddy green in last st, turn.

Rows 7–82: [Rep rows 3–6 consecutively] 19 times.

Rows 83 & 84: Rep rows 3 and 4. At end of last row, fasten off green.

Row 85: Ch 1, sc in each st across, turn.

Row 86: Ch 1, sc in each st across. Fasten off.

FRINGE

Cut 8 strands each of cherry red and paddy green, each 5 inches in length. Holding 1 strand of each color tog, fold in half, pull fold through st, pull ends through fold. Pull to tighten.

Attach Fringe in each st and ch on each short end.

Tie Scarf around neck.

FINISHING

With sewing thread, sew 2-inch piece of hook-and-loop fastener to outer right Arm and right Foot, and to inner left Arm and left Foot. ∎

St. Nick

SKILL LEVEL

INTERMEDIATE

FINISHED SIZE
16 inches tall sitting, including Hat

MATERIALS
- Red Heart Super Saver medium (worsted) weight yarn (7 oz/364 yds/198g per skein):
  2 skeins #319 cherry red
  3 oz/150yds/85g each #311 white and #724 baby pink
  2 oz/100 yds/57g #312 black
  ½ oz/25 yds/14g #321 gold
- TLC Baby Amoré medium (worsted) weight yarn (5 oz/286 yds/140g per skein):
  1 skein #9001 white
- Aunt Lydia's Classic size 10 crochet cotton (400 yds per ball):
  1 ball #1 white
- Size 7/1.65mm steel crochet hook
- Size H/8/5mm crochet hook or size needed to obtain gauge
- Tapestry needle
- Sewing needle
- Sewing thread
- 30 x 40-inch piece of white flannel or blanket fabric
- Fiberfill
- 4-inch piece of hook-and-loop fastener
- Stitch marker

GAUGE
Size H hook and yarn: 4 sc = 1 inch

PATTERN NOTES
Use size H hook with yarn and size 7 hook with crochet cotton.

Use Red Heart Super Saver white yarn for Blanket, Hat, Coat, Legs and Arms.

Use TLC Baby Amoré white yarn for all facial features that use white.

Join with slip stitch as indicated unless otherwise stated.

Work in continuous rounds, do not turn or join unless otherwise stated.

Mark first stitch of each round.

Chain-2 at beginning of row or round counts as first half double crochet unless otherwise stated.

INSTRUCTIONS
BLANKET
Rnd 1: Working around outer edge of fabric, using **size 7 hook** (*see Pattern Notes*), pushing hook through fabric ¼ inch from edge of fabric and with sts ¼ inch apart, join crochet cotton with sc near 1 corner, *evenly sp (ch 2, sc) across until you have even number of ch sps along side to next corner, ch 4 for corner, rep from * around, **join** (*see Pattern Notes*) in beg sc. Fasten off.

Rnd 2: With **size H hook** (*see Pattern Notes*), join **white** (*see Pattern Notes*) with sc in any corner ch-4 sp, sc in same ch sp, sc in each ch-2 sp around with 3 sc in each corner ch-4 sp, sc in same corner ch sp as beg sc, join in beg sc.

Rnd 3: Ch 1, sc in first st, ch 2, sk next st, [sc in next st, ch 2, sk next st] around, join in beg sc. Fasten off.

Rnd 4: Working in sk sts, join cherry red with sc in any sk st in front of ch-2 sp, *ch 2, working behind ch-2 on last rnd, sc in next sk st, ch 2**, working in front of next ch-2 sp, sc in next sk st, rep from * around, ending last rep at **, join in beg sc. Fasten off.

SANTA
HEAD

Rnd 1: Beg at top, with baby pink, ch 2, 6 sc in 2nd ch from hook, **do not join** (*see Pattern Notes*). (*6 sc*)

Rnd 2: 2 sc in each st around. (*12 sc*)

Rnd 3: [Sc in next st, 2 sc in next st] around. (*18 sc*)

Rnd 4: [Sc in each of next 2 sts, 2 sc in next st] around. (*24 sc*)

Rnd 5: [2 sc in next st, sc in each of next 3 sts] around. (*30 sc*)

Rnd 6: [Sc in each of next 4 sts, 2 sc in next st] around. (*36 sc*)

Rnd 7: [Sc in each of next 5 sts, 2 sc in next st] around. (*42 sc*)

Rnd 8: Sc in each st around.

Rnd 9: [Sc in each of next 6 sts, 2 sc in next st] around. (*48 sc*)

Rnd 10: Sc in each st around.

Rnd 11: [Sc in each of next 11 sts, 2 sc in next st] around. (*52 sc*)

Rnds 12–23: Sc in each st around.

Rnd 24: [Sc in each of next 11 sts, **sc dec** (*see Stitch Guide*) in next 2 sts] around. Stuff Head. (*48 sc*)

Rnd 25: [Sc in each of next 4 sts, sc dec in next 2 sts] around. (*40 sc*)

Rnd 26: [Sc in each of next 3 sts, sc dec in next 2 sts] around. Finish stuffing Head. (*32 sc*)

Rnd 27: [Sc in each of next 2 sts, sc dec in next 2 sts] around, join in beg sc. Leaving long end, fasten off. (*24 sc*)

BODY

Rnd 1: Beg at neck, with cherry red, ch 24, sc in first ch to form ring, sc in each ch around, **do not join**. (*24 sc*)

Rnd 2: [Sc in next st, 2 sc in next st] around. (*36 sc*)

Rnd 3: [Sc in each of next 3 sts, 2 sc in next st] around. (*45 sc*)

Rnd 4: Sc in each st around.

Rnd 5: [Sc in each of next 4 sts, 2 sc in next st] around. (*54 sc*)

Rnd 6: Sc in each st around.

Rnd 7: [Sc in each of next 8 sts, 2 sc in next st] around. (*60 sc*)

Rnds 8–15: Sc in each st around.

Rnd 16: Sc in each st around, join in beg sc.

Rnd 17: Working in **back lps** (*see Stitch Guide*), ch 1, sc in each st around, **do not join**.

Rnds 18–34: Sc in each st around.

Rnd 35: [Sc in each of next 4 sts, sc dec in next 2 sts] around. (*50 sc*)

Rnd 36: [Sc in each of next 3 sts, sc dec in next 2 sts] around. Stuff Body. (*40 sc*)

Rnd 37: [Sc in each of next 2 sts, sc dec in next 2 sts] around. (*30 sc*)

Rnd 38: [Sc in each of next 3 sts, sc dec in next 2 sts] around. (*24 sc*)

Rnd 39: [Sc in each of next 2 sts, sc dec in next 2 sts] around. (*18 sc*)

Rnd 40: [Sc in next st, sc dec in next 2 sts] around. Finish stuffing Body. (*12 sc*)

Rnd 41: [Sc dec in next 2 sts] around, join in beg sc. Leaving long end, fasten off. (*6 sc*)

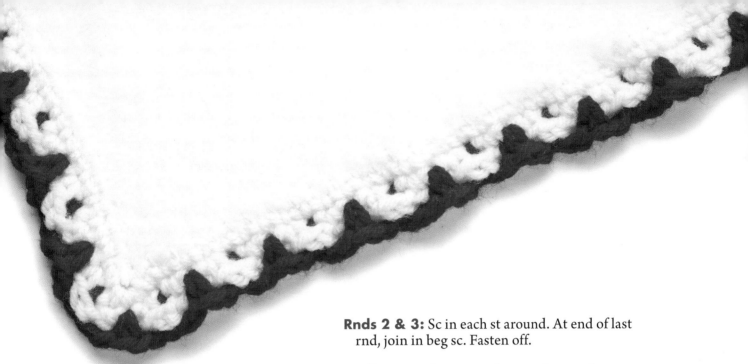

Weave long end through top of sts of last rnd, pull to close. Secure end.

COAT SKIRT
Row 1: With neck facing, working in rem lps on rnd 16 of Body, join cherry red in st at center front, **ch 2** *(see Pattern Notes)*, hdc in same st, hdc in each of next 2 sts, 2 hdc in next st, [hdc in each of next 5 sts, 2 hdc in next st] around to last 2 sts, hdc in next st, 2 hdc in last st, turn. *(72 hdc)*

Rows 2 & 3: Ch 2, hdc in each st across, turn.

Row 4: Ch 2, hdc in each st across. Fasten off.

COAT SKIRT TRIM
Working in ends of rows and in sts, join white in top corner of left side of Coat Skirt, ch 1, hdc in same st, evenly sp 5 sc in ends of rows across, working in sts, 3 hdc in first st, hdc in each st across with 3 hdc in last st, evenly sp 6 hdc in ends of rows. Fasten off.

FRONT TRIM
With white, ch 18, hdc in 3rd ch from hook and in each ch across. Fasten off.

Sew Front Trim to center front of Body above Coat Skirt.

Sew Head to Body.

NOSE
Rnd 1: With cherry red, ch 2, 6 sc in 2nd ch from hook, **do not join.** *(6 sc)*

Rnds 2 & 3: Sc in each st around. At end of last rnd, join in beg sc. Fasten off.

Stuff Nose and sew to rnds 20 and 21 on front of Head.

Using **satin stitch** *(see Fig. 1)*, with black, embroider eyes above Nose 1½ inches apart over rnds 16–18 of Head.

BEARD
With **white** *(see Pattern Notes)*, ch 28, (sl st, {ch 21, sc} twice) in 2nd ch from hook, [ch 21 (sc, ch 21, sc) in next ch] across. Fasten off. Sew Beard to Head, framing face as shown in photo.

Fig. 1
Satin Stitch

EYEBROW
MAKE 2.
With white, ch 9, sl st in 2nd ch from hook and in each ch across. Fasten off.

Sew 1 Eyebrow above each eye as shown in photo.

MOUSTACHE
SIDE
MAKE 2.
With white, ch 7, sl st in 2nd ch from hook, sl st in next ch, sc in next ch, sk next 2 chs, (3 hdc, ch 2, sl st) in last ch. Fasten off.

Tack round part of each Moustache section under Nose, reversing the Side on the right side so that the WS is facing up.

HAIR
With white, ch 35, (sl st, {ch 21, sl st} twice) in 2nd ch from hook, [ch 21, (sc, ch 21, sc) in next ch] across. Fasten off.

Sew ends of Hair strip at sides of Head near Beard, then sew strip down sides of Head along rnd 17 at back of Head.

COLLAR

With white, ch 33, 3 dc in 4th ch from hook, dc in each of next 28 chs, (3 dc, ch 2, sl st) in last ch. Fasten off.

Sew Collar around neck with ends in front.

BELT

Row 1: With black, ch 3, sc in 2nd ch from hook and in last ch, turn. *(2 sc)*

Rows 2–46: Ch 1, sc in each st across, turn.

Row 47: Ch 1, sc in each st across. Fasten off.

Place Belt around waist, overlapping at center front, sew in place.

BUCKLE

With gold, ch 13, sl st in 2nd ch from hook, sl st in next ch, (sl st, ch 1, sl st) in next ch *(corner)*, [sl st in each of next 2 chs, (sl st, ch 1, sl st) in next ch *(corner)*] around, join in beg sl st. Fasten off.

Sew Buckle over ends of Belt at center front.

HAT

Rnd 1: Beg at bottom edge, with cherry red, ch 54, join with sc in first ch to form ring, sc in each ch around, **do not join.** *(54 sc)*

Rnds 2–8: Sc in each st around.

Rnd 9: [Sc in each of next 25 sts, sc dec in next 2 sts] around. *(52 sc)*

Rnd 10: Sc in each st around.

Rnd 11: [Sc in each of next 11 sts, sc dec in next 2 sts] around. *(48 sc)*

Rnd 12: Sc in each st around.

Rnd 13: [Sc in each of next 10 sts, sc dec in next 2 sts] around. *(44 sc)*

Rnds 14 & 15: Sc in each st around.

Rnd 16: [Sc in each of next 9 sts, sc dec in next 2 sts] around. *(40 sc)*

Rnd 17: Sc in each st around.

Rnd 18: [Sc in each of next 8 sts, sc dec in next 2 sts] around. *(36 sc)*

Rnd 19: [Sc in each of next 7 sts, sc dec in next 2 sts] around. *(32 sc)*

Rnd 20: [Sc in each of next 6 sts, sc dec in next 2 sts] around. *(28 sc)*

Rnd 21: Sc in each st around.

Rnd 22: [Sc in each of next 5 sts, sc dec in next 2 sts] around. *(24 sc)*

Rnd 23: Sc in each st around.

Rnd 24: [Sc in each of next 4 sts, sc dec in next 2 sts] around. *(20 sc)*

Rnd 25: Sc in each st around.

Rnd 26: [Sc in each of next 3 sts, sc dec in next 2 sts] around. *(16 sc)*

Rnd 27: Sc in each st around.

Rnd 28: [Sc in each of next 2 sts, sc dec in next 2 sts] around. *(12 sc)*

Rnd 29: Sc in each st around.

Rnds 30 & 31: Rep rnds 28 and 29. *(9 sc at end of last rnd)*

Rnd 32: [Sc in next st, sc dec in next st] around. *(6 sc)*

Rnd 33: Sc in each st around, join in beg sc. Fasten off.

POMPOM

Rnd 1: With white, ch 2, 4 sc in 2nd ch from hook, **do not join.** *(4 sc)*

Rnd 2: 2 sc in each st around. *(8 sc)*

Rnds 3 & 4: Sc in each st around. Stuff.

Rnd 5: [Sk next st, sl st in next st] around. Fasten off.

Sew to tip of Hat.

HAT TRIM

Rnd 1: Working in starting ch on opposite side of rnd 1 on Hat, join white with sc in any ch, sc in each ch around, join in beg sc. *(54 sc)*

Rnd 2: Working in back lps, ch 2, hdc in each of next 7 sts, 2 hdc in next st, [hdc in each of next 8 sts, 2 hdc in next st] around, join in 2nd ch of beg ch-2. *(60 hdc)*

Rnd 3: Ch 1, sc in each st around, join in beg sc. Fasten off.

Sew rnd 1 of Hat to top of Head as shown in photo.

ARM
MAKE 2.

Rnd 1: Beg at top, with cherry red, ch 20, sc in first ch to form ring, sc in each ch around, **do not join**. *(20 sc)*

Rnds 2–27: Sc in each st around. At end of last rnd, join with sl st in beg sc. Fasten off.

CUFF

Rnd 28: Join white with sc in first st, sc in each st around, join in beg sc, **turn**.

Rnd 29: Working in back lps, ch 2, hdc in each of next 3 sts, 2 hdc in next st, [hdc in each of next 4 sts, 2 hdc in next st] around, join in 2nd ch of beg ch-2. *(24 hdc)*

Rnd 30: Ch 1, sc in each st around, join in beg sc. Fasten off.

Fold Cuff up over Arm.

HAND

Rnd 1: Working in rem lps of rnd 28, join baby pink with sc in first st, sc in each of next 2 sts, [2 sc in next st, sc in next st] 4 times, sc in each st around, **do not join**. *(24 sc)*

Rnds 2–6: Sc in each st around.

Rnd 7: [Sc in each of next 2 sts, sc dec in next 2 sts] around. *(18 sc)*

Rnd 8: [Sc in next st, sc dec in next 2 sts] around. *(12 sc)*

Rnd 9: [Sc dec in next 2 sts] around. Leaving long end, fasten off. *(6 sc)*

Weave long end through top of sts on last rnd, pull to close. Secure end.

Stuff Arm lightly, leaving the top 2 inches unstuffed.

Flatten rnd 1 and sew closed.

Sew Arms to sides of Body as shown in photo.

LEG
MAKE 2.

Rnds 1–30: Rep rnds 1–30 of Arm.

FOOT

Rnds 1–9: With black, rep rnds 1–9 of Hand.

Weave long end through top of sts on last rnd, pull to close. Secure end.

Stuff Leg lightly, leaving the top 2 inches unstuffed.

Flatten rnd 1 and sew closed.

Sew Legs to sides of Body as shown in photo.

FINISHING

With sewing thread, sew 2-inch piece of hook-and-loop fastener to outer right Hand and right Foot, and to inner left Hand and left Foot. ∎

Stitch Guide
For more complete information, visit **FreePatterns.com**

ABBREVIATIONS

beg	begin/begins/beginning
bpdc	back post double crochet
bpsc	back post single crochet
bptr	back post treble crochet
CC	contrasting color
ch(s)	chain(s)
ch-	refers to chain or space previously made (e.g., ch-1 space)
ch sp(s)	chain space(s)
cl(s)	cluster(s)
cm	centimeter(s)
dc	double crochet (singular/plural)
dc dec	double crochet 2 or more stitches together, as indicated
dec	decrease/decreases/decreasing
dtr	double treble crochet
ext	extended
fpdc	front post double crochet
fpsc	front post single crochet
fptr	front post treble crochet
g	gram(s)
hdc	half double crochet
hdc dec	half double crochet 2 or more stitches together, as indicated
inc	increase/increases/increasing
lp(s)	loop(s)
MC	main color
mm	millimeter(s)
oz	ounce(s)
pc	popcorn(s)
rem	remain/remains/remaining
rep(s)	repeat(s)
rnd(s)	round(s)
RS	right side
sc	single crochet (singular/plural)
sc dec	single crochet 2 or more stitches together, as indicated
sk	skip/skipped/skipping
sl st(s)	slip stitch(es)
sp(s)	space/spaces/spaced
st(s)	stitch(es)
tog	together
tr	treble crochet
trtr	triple treble
WS	wrong side
yd(s)	yard(s)
yo	yarn over

Chain—ch: Yo, pull through lp on hook.

Slip stitch—sl st: Insert hook in st, pull through both lps on hook.

Single crochet—sc: Insert hook in st, yo, pull through st, yo, pull through both lps on hook.

Front post stitch—fp: Back post stitch—bp: When working post st, insert hook from right to left around post st on previous row.

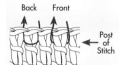

Front loop—front lp Back loop—back lp

Front Loop Back Loop

Half double crochet—hdc: Yo, insert hook in st, yo, pull through st, yo, pull through all 3 lps on hook.

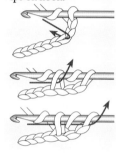

Double crochet—dc: Yo, insert hook in st, yo, pull through st, [yo, pull through 2 lps] twice.

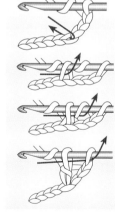

Change colors: Drop first color; with 2nd color, pull through last 2 lps of st.

Treble crochet—tr: Yo twice, insert hook in st, yo, pull through st, [yo, pull through 2 lps] 3 times.

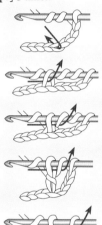

Double treble crochet—dtr: Yo 3 times, insert hook in st, yo, pull through st, [yo, pull through 2 lps] 4 times.

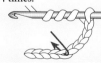

Single crochet decrease (sc dec): (Insert hook, yo, draw lp through) in each of the sts indicated, yo, draw through all lps on hook.

Example of 2-sc dec

Half double crochet decrease (hdc dec): (Yo, insert hook, yo, draw lp through) in each of the sts indicated, yo, draw through all lps on hook.

Example of 2-hdc dec

Double crochet decrease (dc dec): (Yo, insert hook, yo, draw loop through, draw through 2 lps on hook) in each of the sts indicated, yo, draw through all lps on hook.

Example of 2-dc dec

Treble crochet decrease (tr dec): Holding back last lp of each st, tr in each of the sts indicated, yo, pull through all lps on hook.

Example of 2-tr dec

US		UK
sl st (slip stitch)	=	sc (single crochet)
sc (single crochet)	=	dc (double crochet)
hdc (half double crochet)	=	htr (half treble crochet)
dc (double crochet)	=	tr (treble crochet)
tr (treble crochet)	=	dtr (double treble crochet)
dtr (double treble crochet)	=	ttr (triple treble crochet)
skip	=	miss

Metric Conversion Charts

INCHES INTO MILLIMETRES & CENTIMETRES (Rounded off slightly)

inches	mm	cm	inches	cm	inches	cm	inches	cm
1/8	3	0.3	5	12.5	21	53.5	38	96.5
1/4	6	0.6	5 1/2	14	22	56	39	99
3/8	10	1	6	15	23	58.5	40	101.5
1/2	13	1.3	7	18	24	61	41	104
5/8	15	1.5	8	20.5	25	63.5	42	106.5
3/4	20	2	9	23	26	66	43	109
7/8	22	2.2	10	25.5	27	68.5	44	112
1	25	2.5	11	28	28	71	45	114.5
1 1/4	32	3.2	12	30.5	29	73.5	46	117
1 1/2	38	3.8	13	33	30	76	47	119.5
1 3/4	45	4.5	14	35.5	31	79	48	122
2	50	5	15	38	32	81.5	49	124.5
2 1/2	65	6.5	16	40.5	33	84	50	127
3	75	7.5	17	43	34	86.5		
3 1/2	90	9	18	46	35	89		
4	100	10	19	48.5	36	91.5		
4 1/2	115	11.5	20	51	37	94		

METRIC CONVERSIONS

yards	x	.9144	=	metres (m)
yards	x	91.44	=	centimetres (cm)
inches	x	2.54	=	centimetres (cm)
inches	x	25.40	=	millimetres (mm)
inches	x	.0254	=	metres (m)

centimetres	x	.3937	=	inches
metres	x	1.0936	=	yards

KNITTING NEEDLES CONVERSION CHART

Canada/U.S.	0	1	2	3	4	5	6	7	8	9	10	10½	11	13	15
Metric (mm)	2	2¼	2¾	3¼	3½	3¾	4	4½	5	5½	6	6½	8	9	10

CROCHET HOOKS CONVERSION CHART

Canada/U.S.	1/B	2/C	3/D	4/E	5/F	6/G	8/H	9/I	10/J	10½/K	N
Metric (mm)	2.25	2.75	3.25	3.5	3.75	4.25	5	5.5	6	6.5	9.0

TOLL-FREE ORDER LINE or to request a free catalog (800) LV-ANNIE (800) 582-6643
Customer Service (800) AT-ANNIE (800) 282-6643, **Fax** (800) 882-6643
Visit AnniesAttic.com
We have made every effort to ensure the accuracy and completeness of these instructions.
We cannot, however, be responsible for human error, typographical mistakes or variations in individual work.

ISBN: 978-1-59635-262-9

Printed in USA

1 2 3 4 5 6 7 8 9